MAGICAL MANDALAS

COLORING BOOK

By the Illustrator of the *Mystical Mandala Coloring Book*

ALBERTA HUTCHINSON

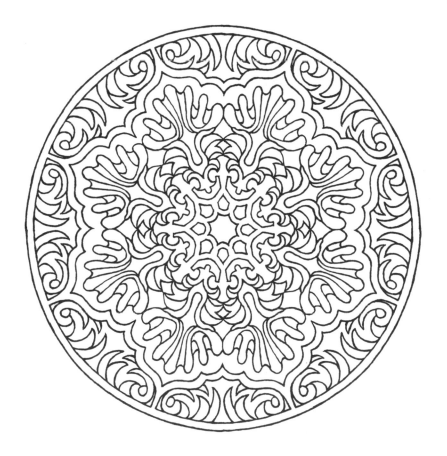

DOVER PUBLICATIONS, INC.
MINEOLA, NEW YORK

Mandalas are symmetrical designs that represent the universe, and are used as a tool for meditation in many cultures. Originally found in the ancient teachings of the Buddhist and Hindu religions, these patterns are recognized throughout the world for their spiritual content as well as their enchanting beauty. Carefully constructed in form and color to evoke feelings of enlightenment, relaxation, and peace, the mandala makes for a unique coloring challenge, perfect for Dover's *Creative Haven* series for the experienced colorist. The thirty-one detailed designs are perfect for experimentation with different media and coloring techniques, plus, the perforated, unbacked pages make displaying finished work easy!

Copyright

Copyright © 2016 by Dover Publications, Inc.
All rights reserved.

Bibliographical Note

Magical Mandalas Coloring Book is a new work,
first published by Dover Publications, Inc., in 2016.

International Standard Book Number

ISBN-13: 978-0-486-79987-2
ISBN-10: 0-486-79987-5

Manufactured in the United States by RR Donnelley
79987501   2016
www.doverpublications.com

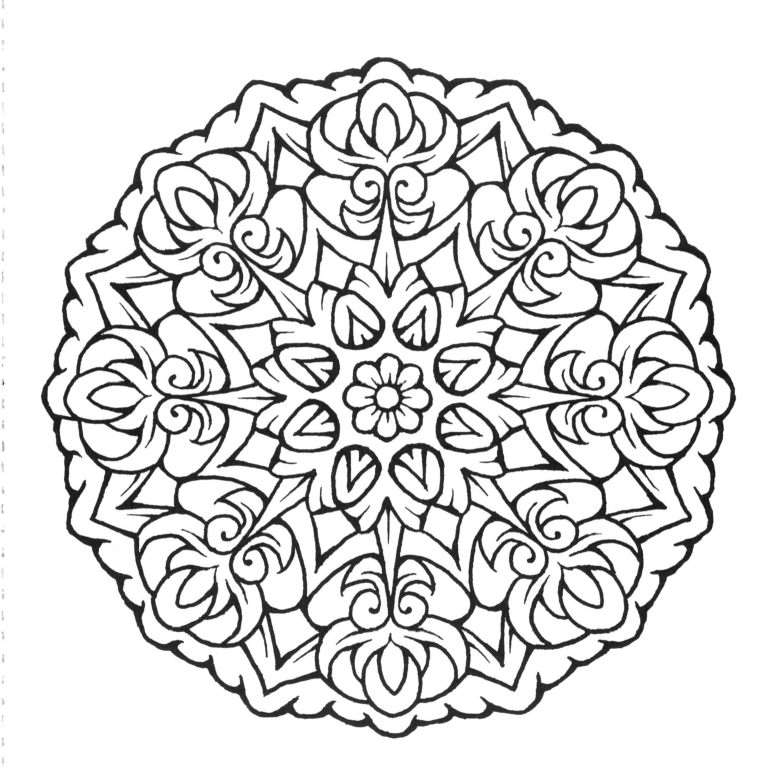

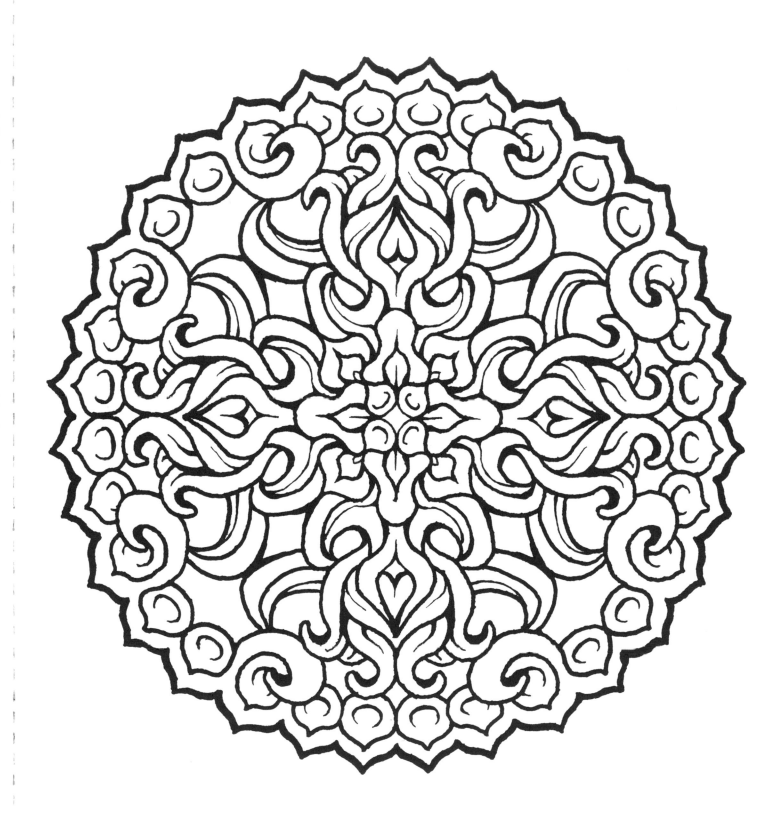

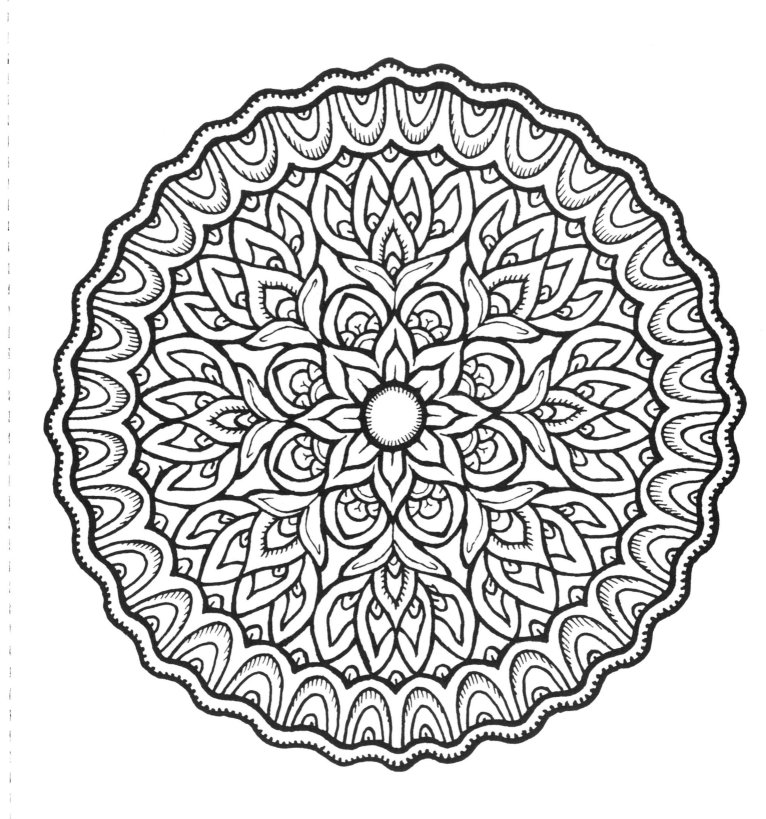

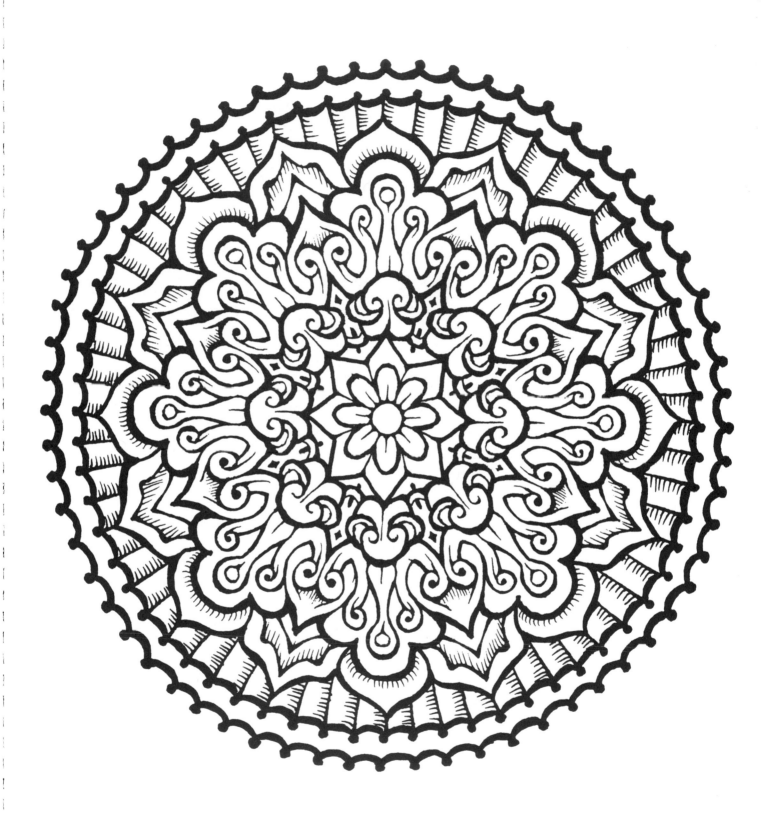

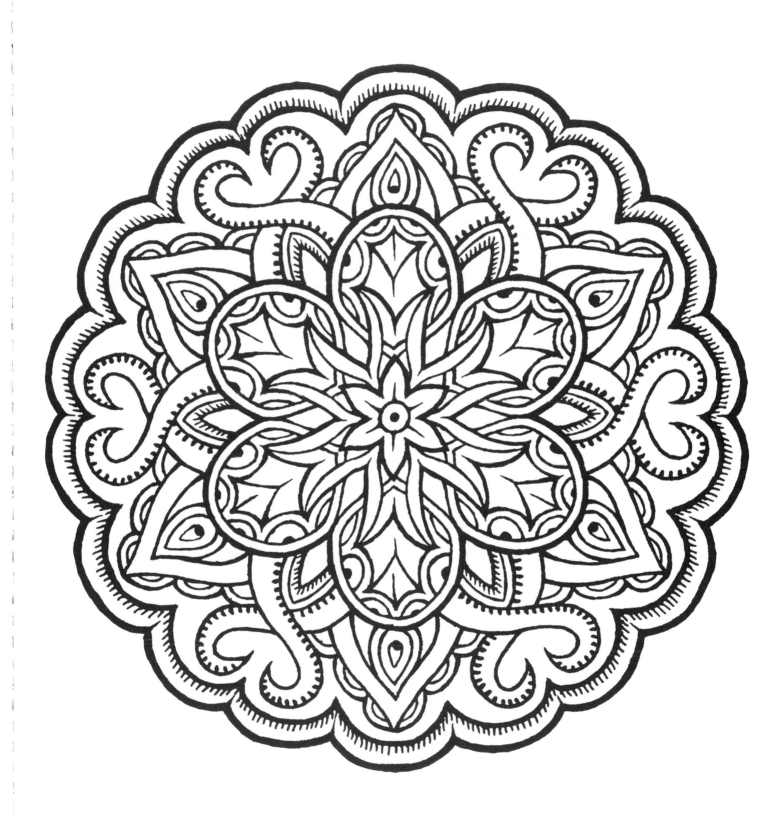

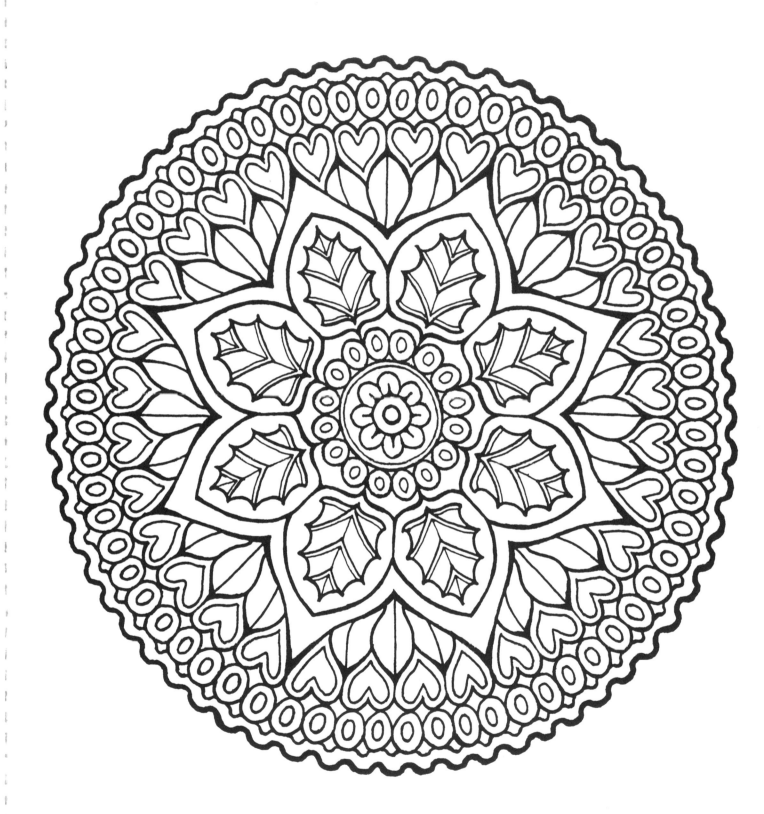

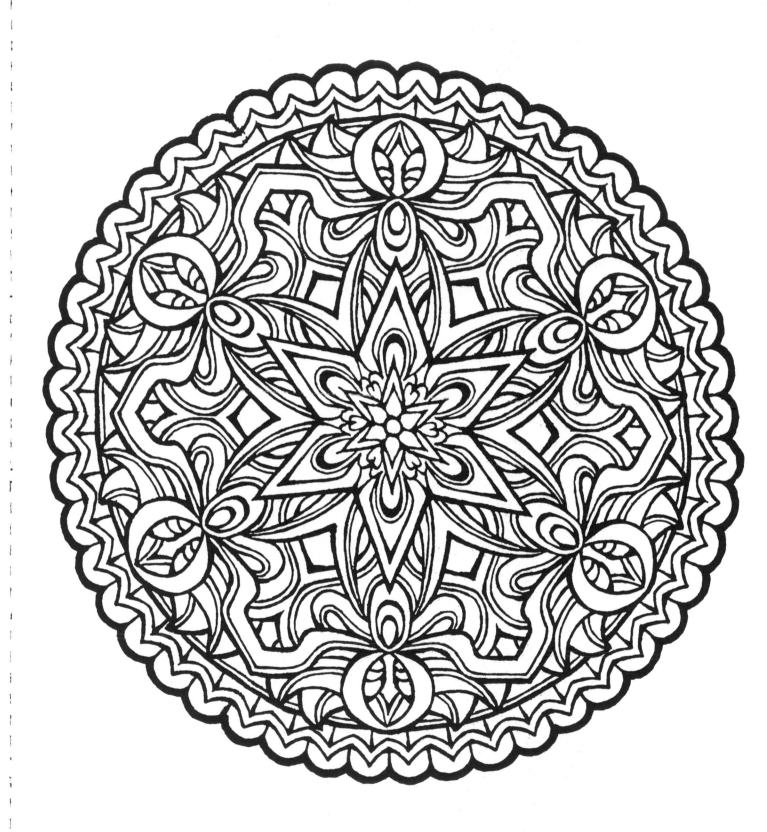

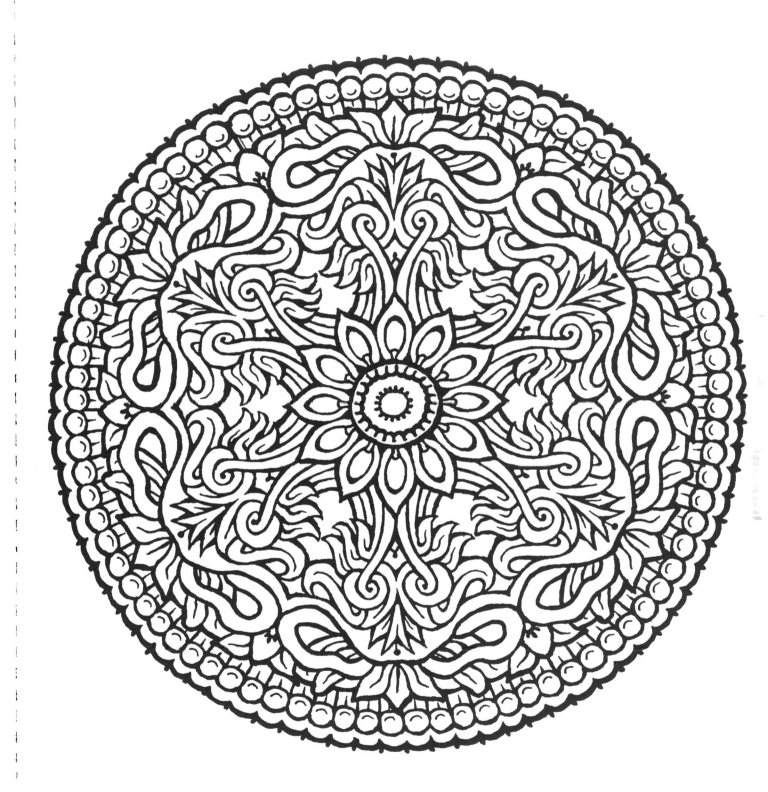

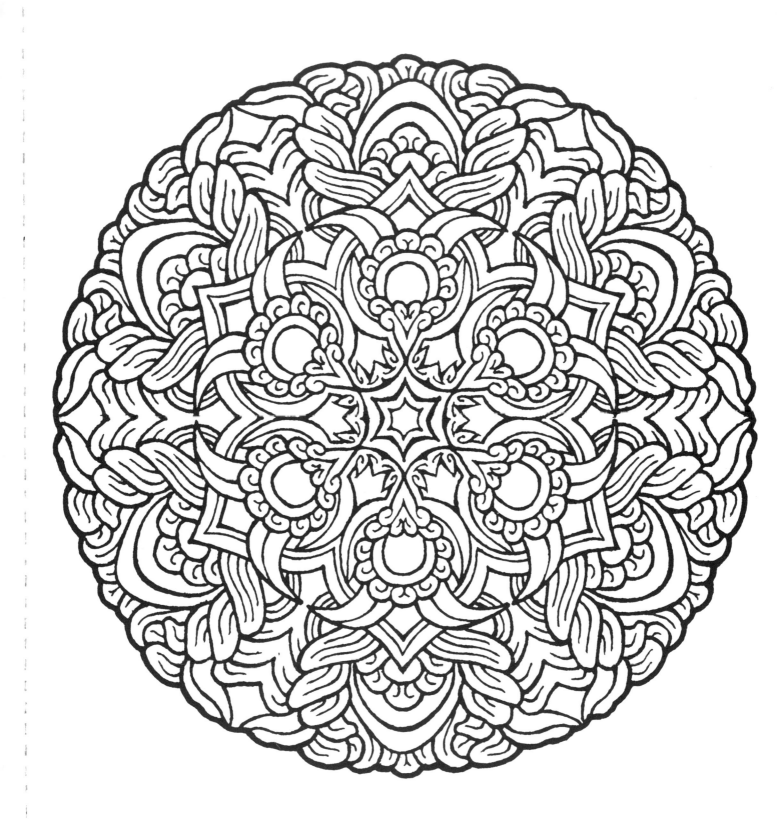

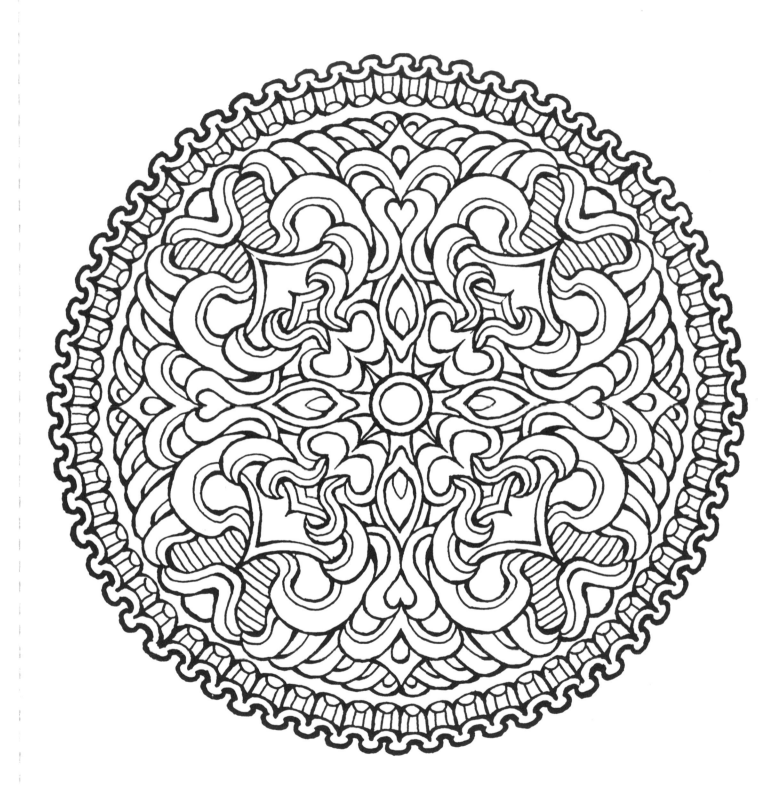

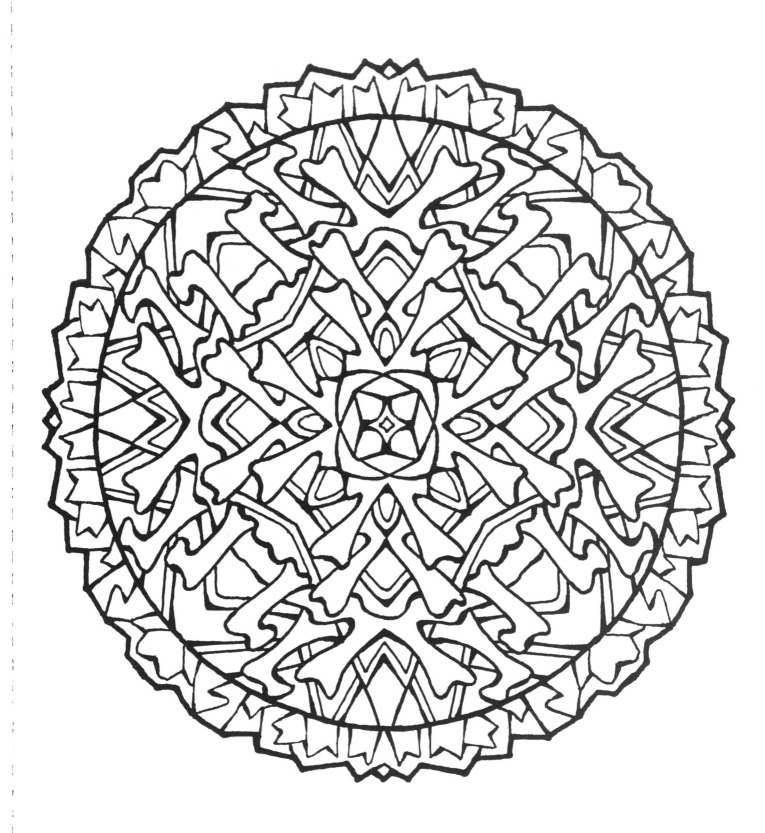

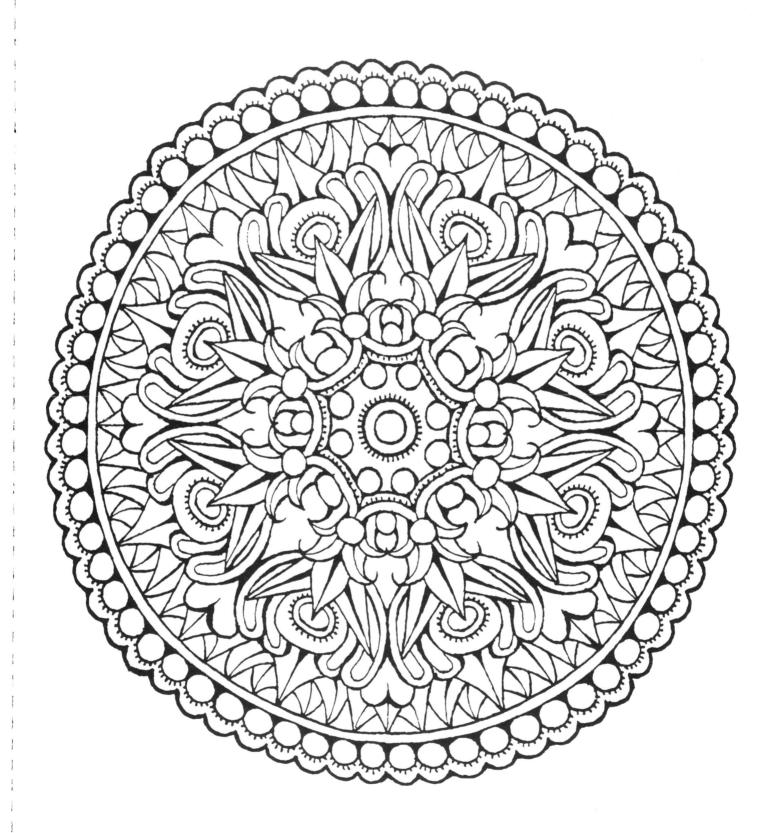

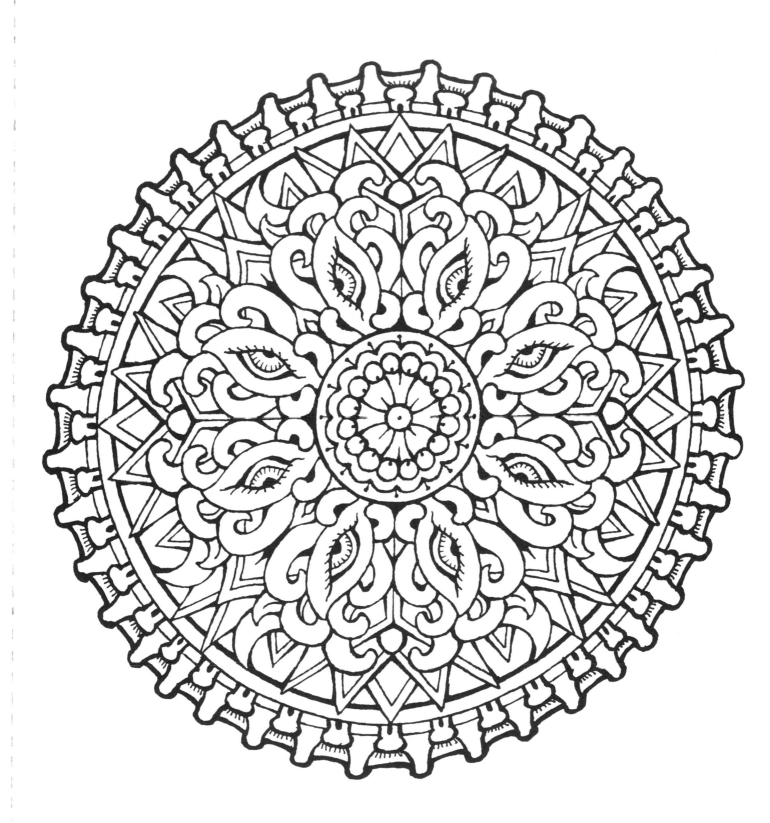

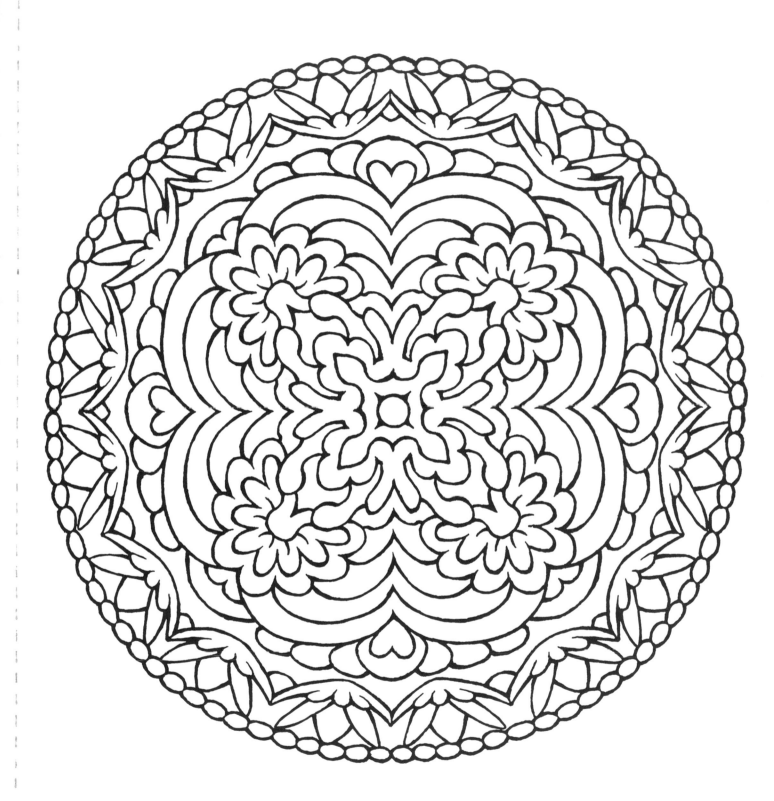

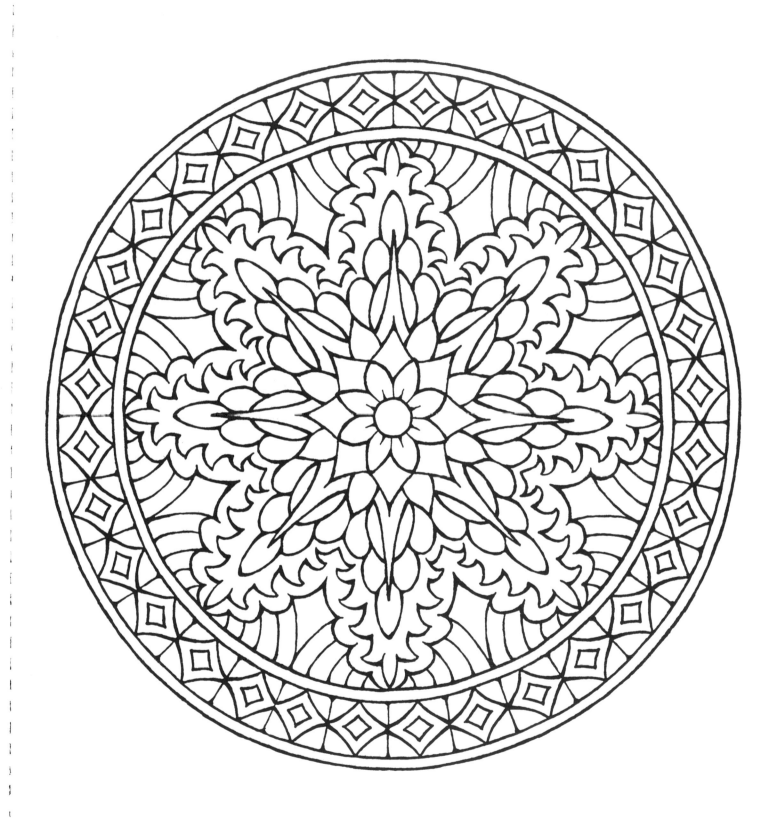

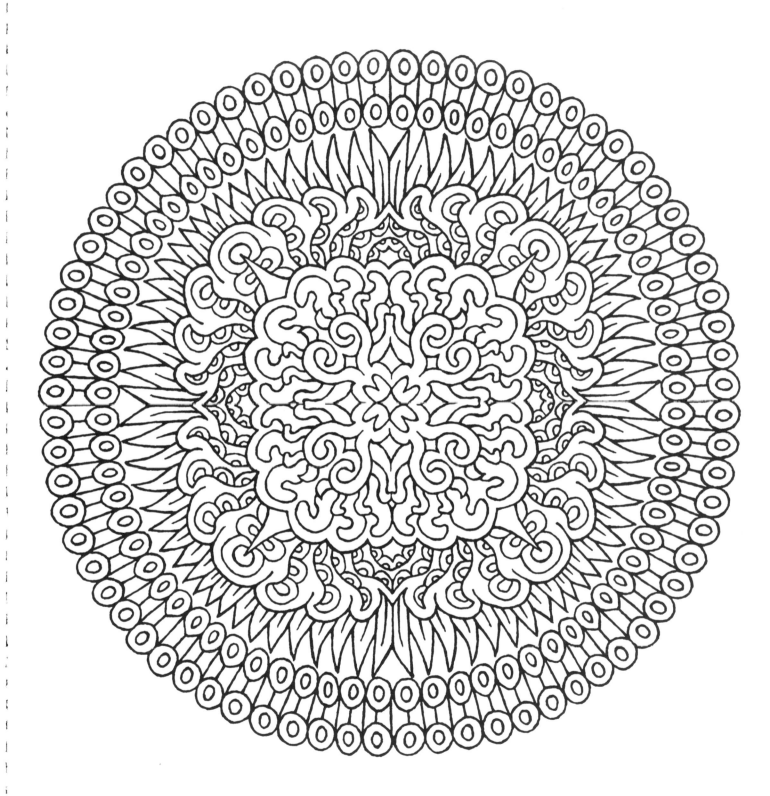

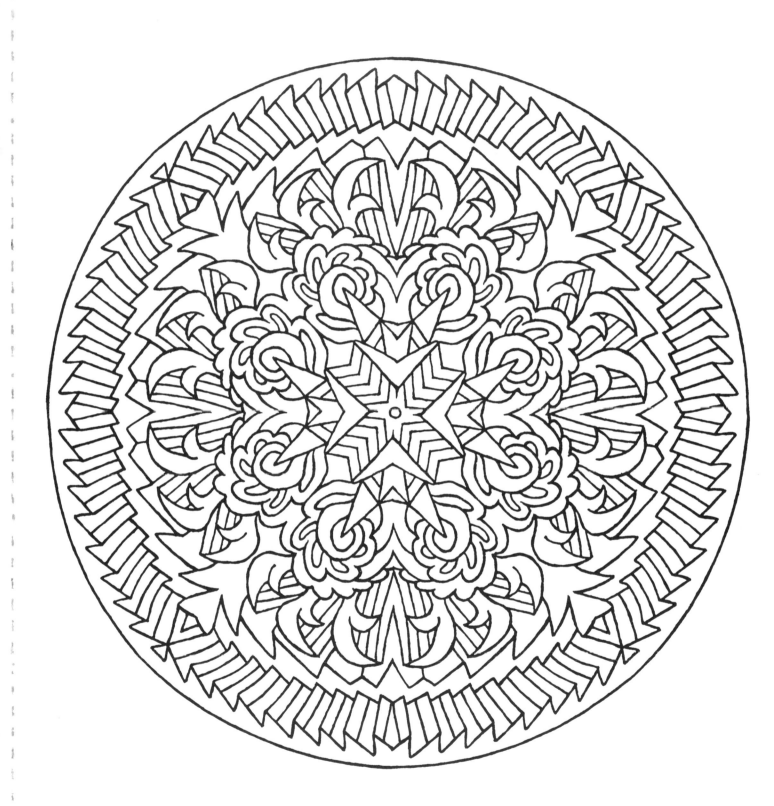

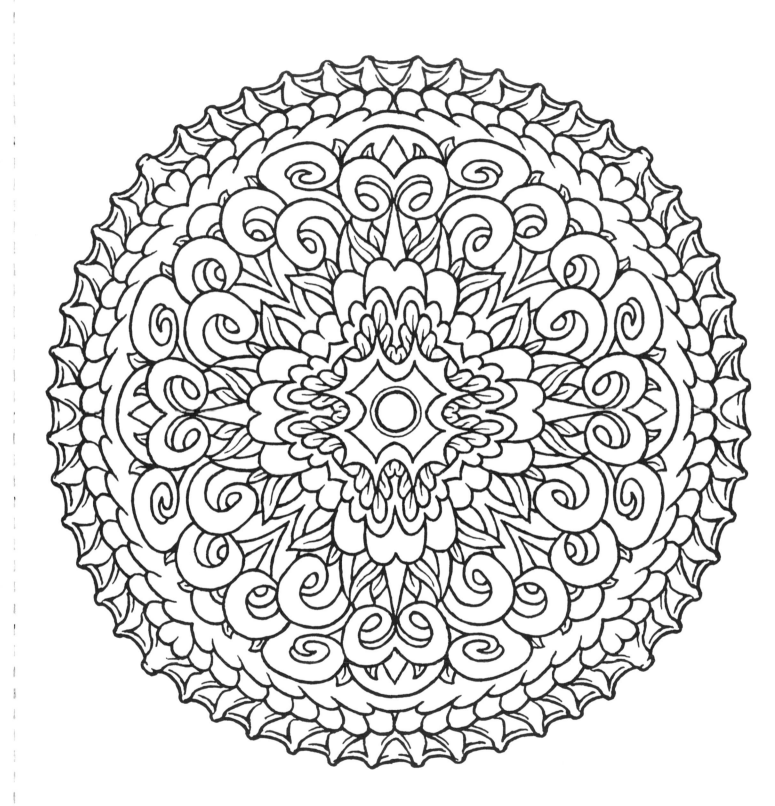

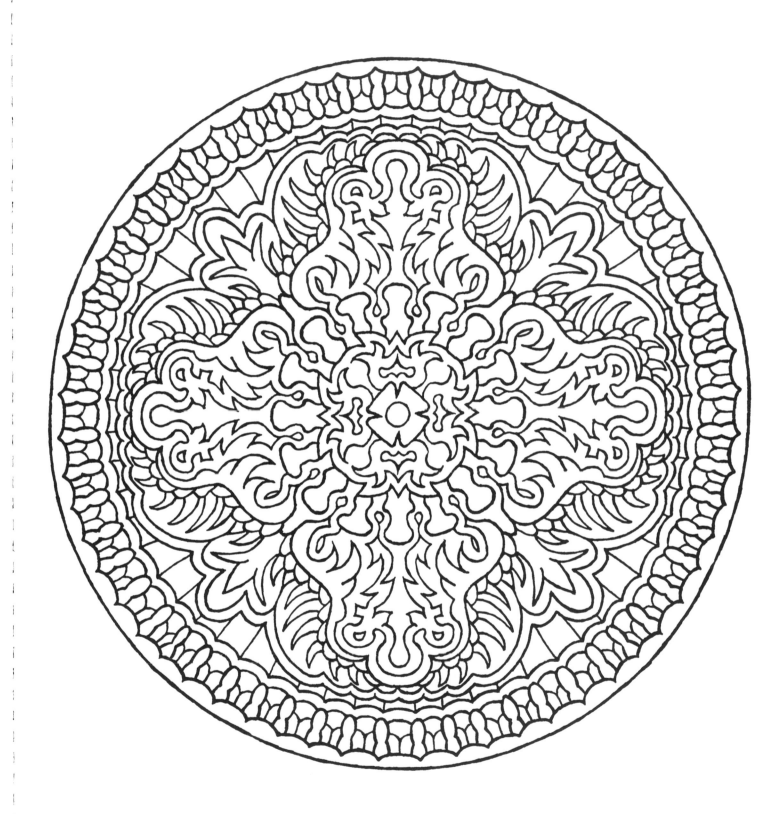

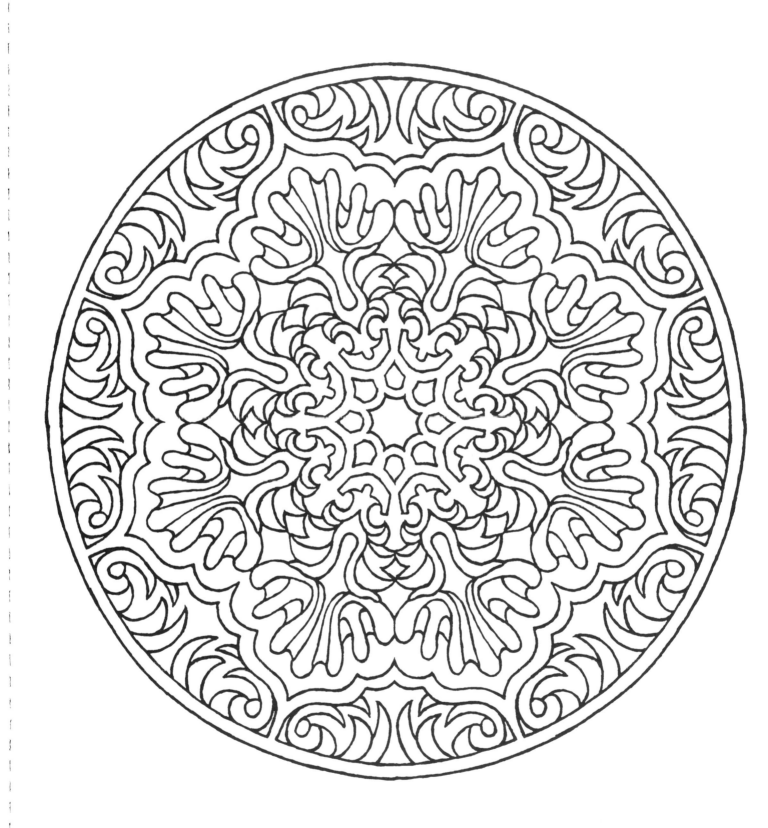

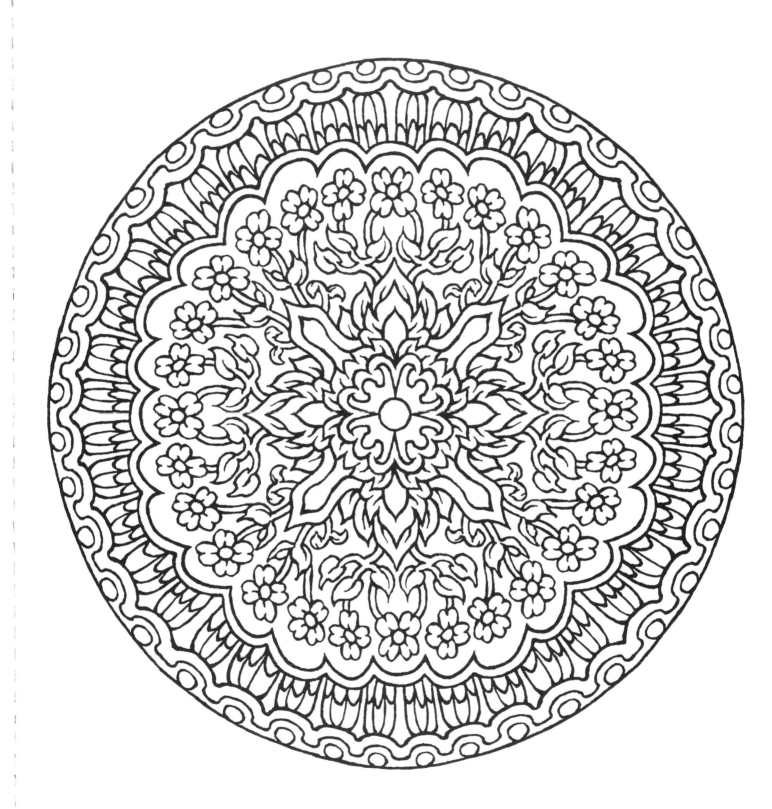

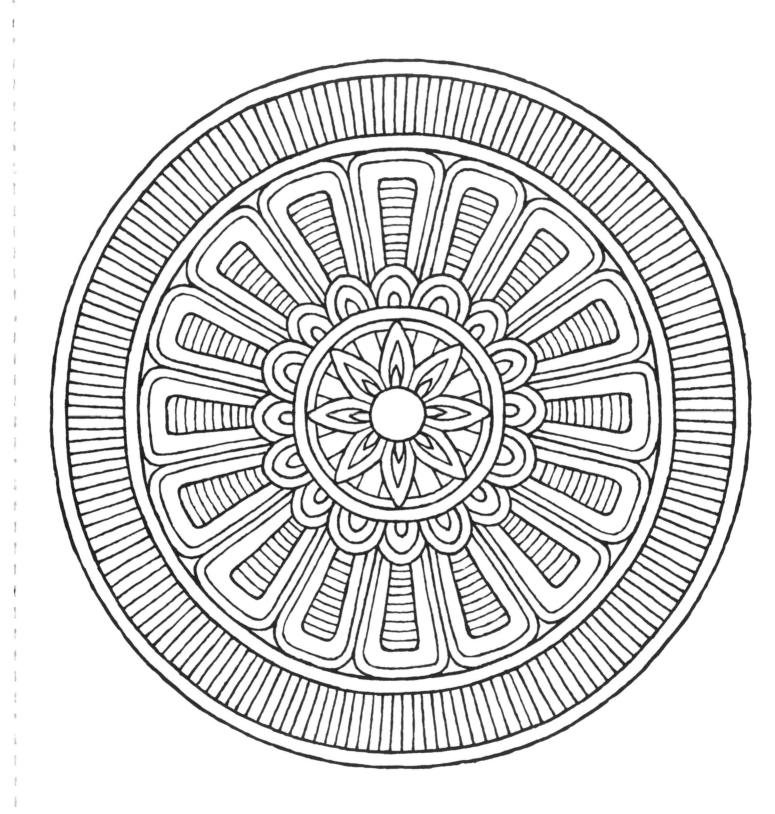

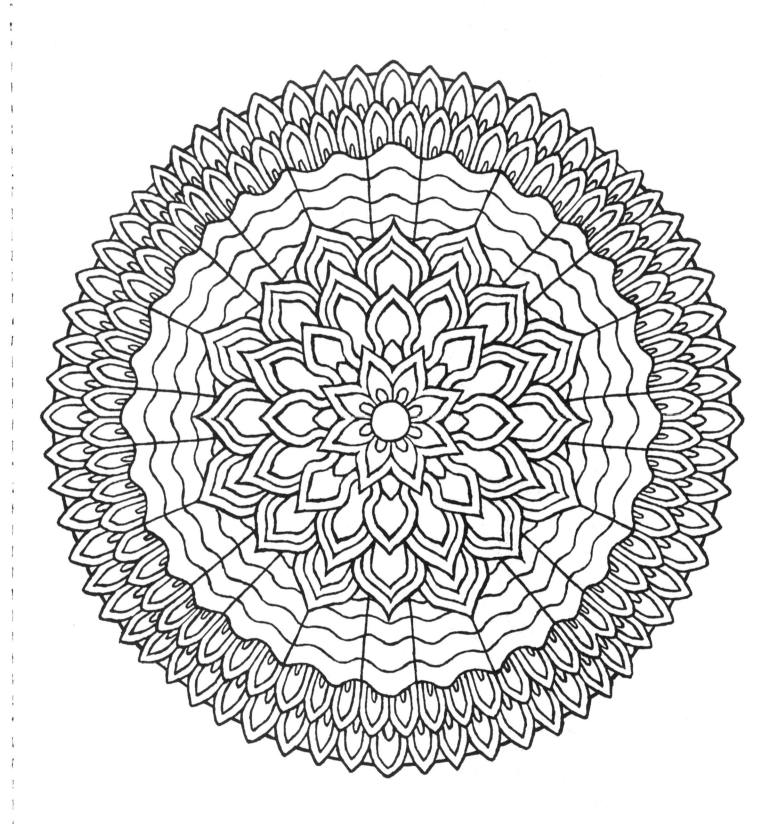

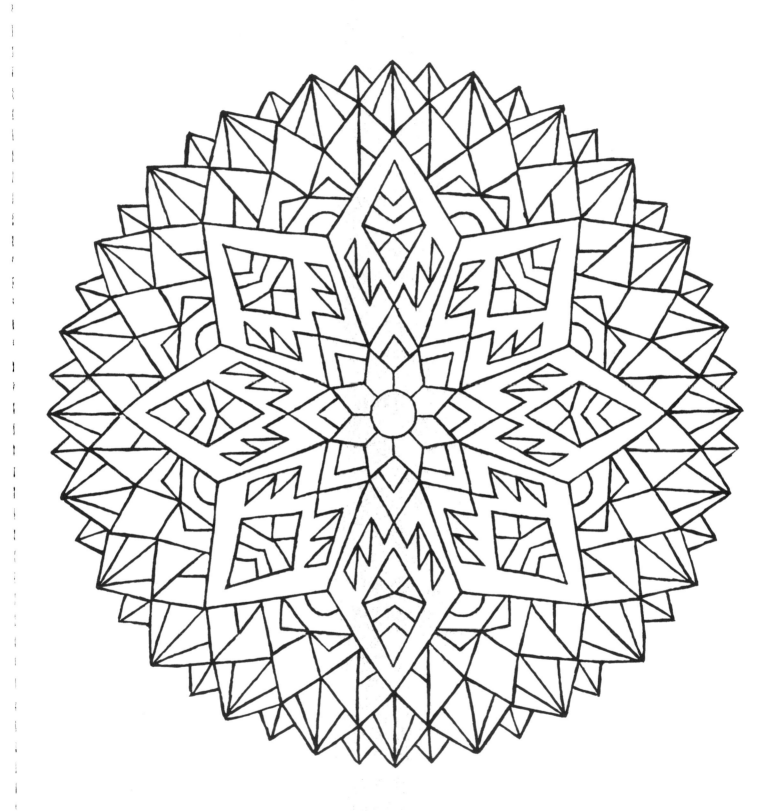

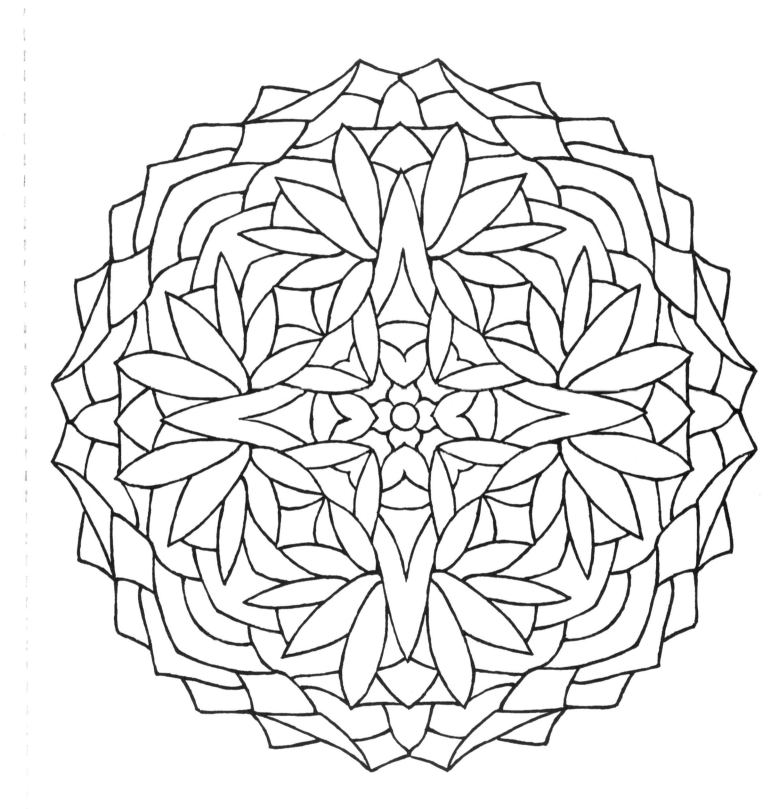

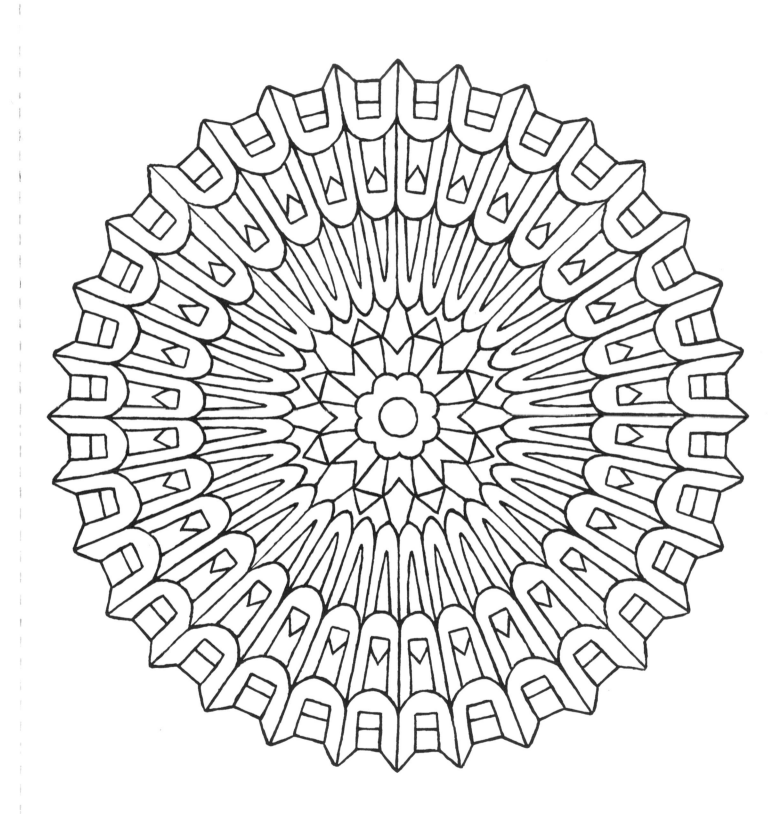

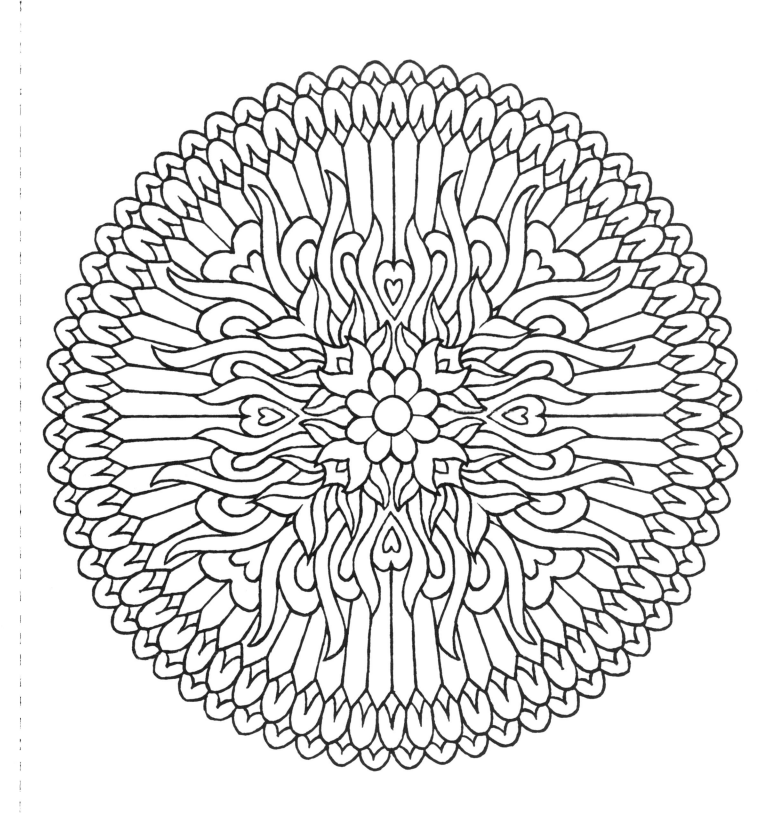

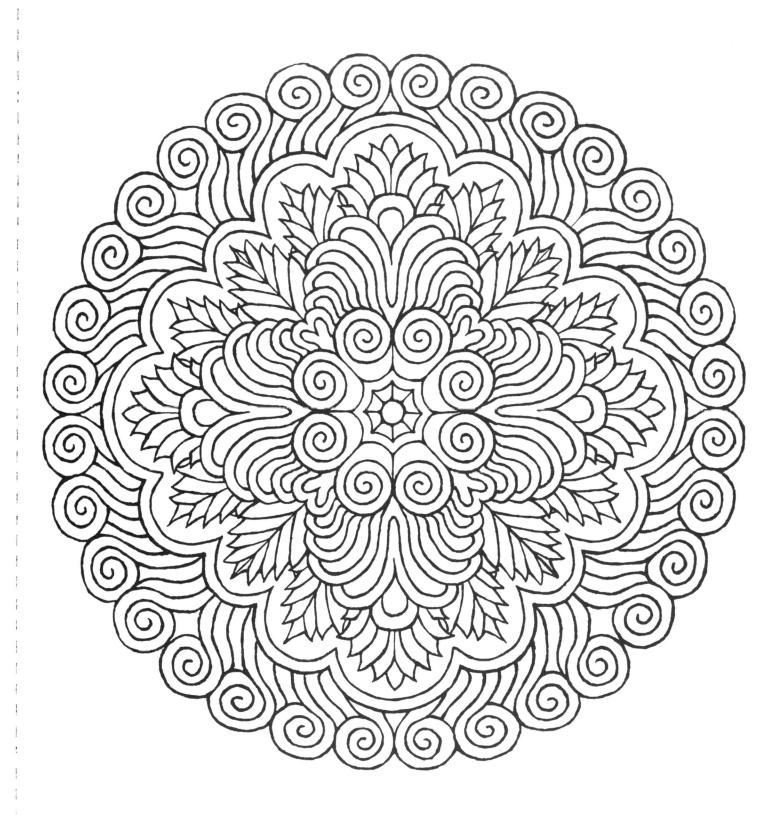

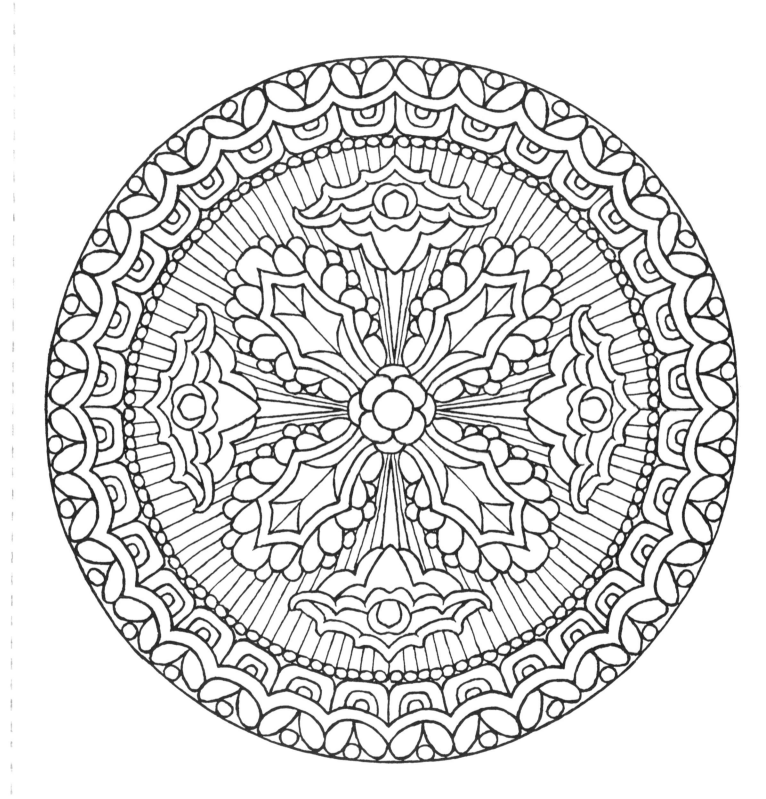

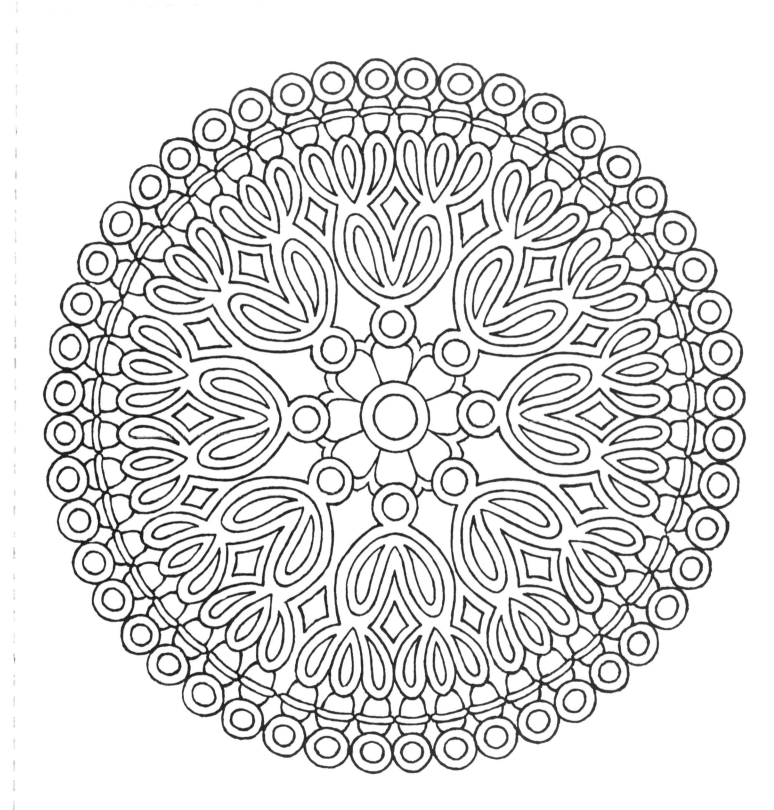

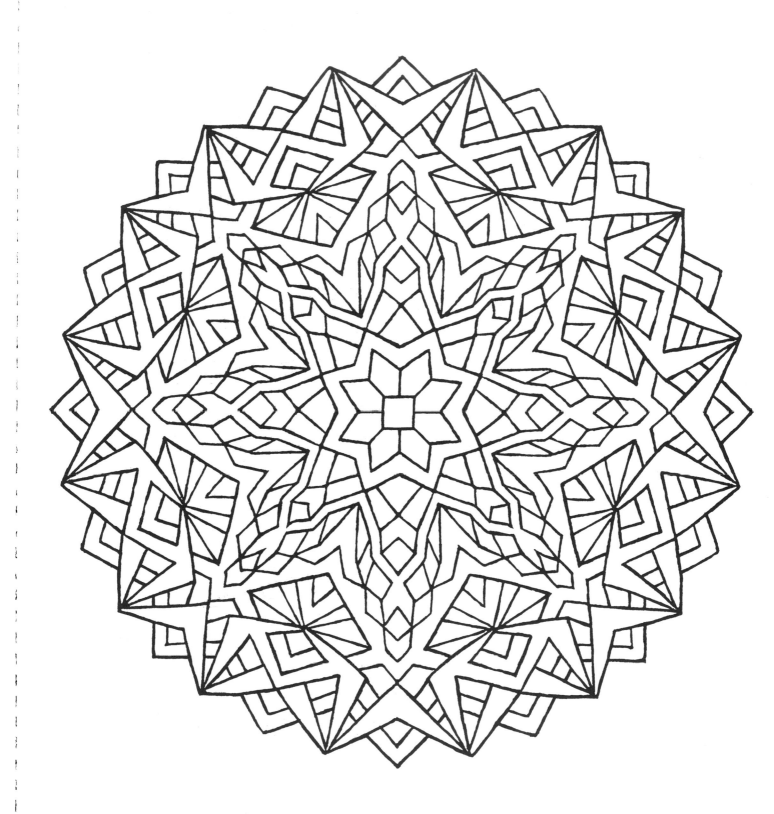